BERNARD SHAW
THROUGH THE CAMERA

BERNARD SHAW

through the Camera

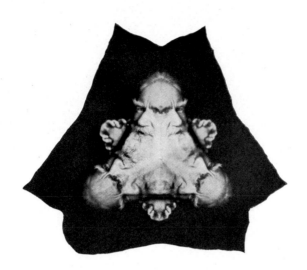

238 photographs, including many taken by Mr. Shaw, selected and introduced by his Bibliographer and Remembrancer

F. E. LOEWENSTEIN

1948

B & H White Publications Ltd.,
23, Fleet Street,
London

Note

The Editor and the Publishers wish to express their thanks to the owners of pictures who have so readily lent them for this book, especially to Mr. Bernard Shaw and his Secretary, Miss Blanche Patch.   They also gratefully acknowledge the constant help and encouragement given by Mr. Ivo L. Currall.

Suggestions from readers, for pictures to be included in future editions of this volume, will be welcomed.

Despite diligent enquiries it has not been possible to trace the photographers of some of the illustrations in this book.

Our apologies are due to those Copyright owners who can substantiate their claims.   On application to the Publishers they will receive the usual fee for reproduction.

Printed in Great Britain by
THE LEAGRAVE PRESS LTD., LUTON, ENGLAND
on paper made by
WIGGINS, TEAPE & ALEX PIRIE (SALES) LTD., LONDON, ENGLAND.

Contents

Introduction

A book of photographs needs no apology : pictures more even than paintings and music are international : they speak for themselves. A collection of Shavian photos may, however, bear a word of explanation from the publisher and the editor. Both are Shaw fans. And there are others everywhere.

The idea of the book was born in the head of a publisher. He asked a few friends for their opinion. Satisfied with the answers he received, he approached the Great Man himself. G.B.S., in the beginning, did not look favorably upon the project. Prospective buyers, he said, would get tired of his face. They would hastily put down the volume; and not only that, would be put off from buying his books. But when our publisher had a few sample pages made, showing not only Shaw and Shaw and Shaw, but Shaw and his contemporaries, and when he pleaded that there was a precedent in the form of a pictorial Life of Goethe, the Great Man relented and, as usual with him, began to advise and help.

I have therefore been able to include photos of his ancestors and his family, from his own collection. As an amateur-photographer himself, and a friend of many eminent photographers, the secrets of the little black magic box are no secrets to him.

Shaw is one of the most photographed men in the world. His face and figure are photogenic and a constant joy to caricaturists. There is no childhood-photo of Shaw. His parents were satisfied with an oleograph of a bonny auburn-haired boy, which was flatteringly like Bob or Sonny, as his father called him. How were they to know that one day a photo might be in great demand? Thus our first photograph is the one taken of him posing with his boyhood-friend, Edward McNulty, in 1874, 2 years before he left on the Shavian *hegira* from Medina-Dublin to London, the modern Mecca.

His adolescence can best be illustrated by these verses, of

9

which the author is unknown. They might have been written
by Lord Olivier or by Charles Burton :

> Shaw golden crowned and ivory faced,
> Moral—but not straightly laced,
> Celt by blood—and Celt in wit,*
> Clever, rather hard to hit,
> Picturesquely economic
> On occasion rather comic—
> Queer in hat—and queer in clothes ;
> What he really thinks who knows ?
> Earnest genius ? Flash of Light ?
> Vegetarian ! Ibsenite !
> Curious compound—nothing more :
> Jaeger clothed non-smoking Shaw.

Look at the images : every one is different, but it is always
the same Shaw, though the biologists try to tell us differently.
Alter et idem as they would have said in Shakespear's time ;
or as Horace said *aliusque et idem*, or as we read in Wordsworth's
poem :

> And in the crystal flood
> Another and the same !

F.E.L.

---

* Shaw repudiates the Celtic Twilight, and insists that he is a Blonde Beast, less an
ancient Roman than a Dane.

BERNARD SHAW

Chief Events and Principal Works

1856   Born 26th July, at 3 Upper Synge Street, now 33 Synge Street, Dublin, third and last child and only son of George Carr Shaw and Lucinda Elizabeth Shaw (née Gurly).

1871   Educated by his governess, Caroline Hill, and at private schools in and near Dublin, he entered on the 1st November the office of Messrs. Charles Uniacke and Thomas Courtney Townshend, Land Agents, of 15 Molesworth Street, Dublin. He made good, and became chief cashier.

1876   At the end of March, however, he burnt his boats, and in April joined his Mother and Lucy, the elder of his two sisters (Agnes, the younger, having just died) at No. 13 Victoria (now Netherton) Grove, Fulham Road, London, S.W.

1876/77   Musical Ghost-Critic to *The Hornet* for Vandaleur Lee.

1878/79   Stayed at home and wrote a novel, which he called *Immaturity*, first published fifty years later in 1930 with a lengthy autobiographical preface. The MS, as well as that of three other novels, was given to the National Library of Ireland in 1946.

1879/80   14th November, joined the staff of *The Edison Telephone Company of London* and was made Manager of the Way-Leave Department, but quitted on its amalgamation with the rival Bell Company on the 7th July, 1880, abandoning commercial employment (this " sin against my nature ") for ever.
Lived for the next five years on his parents, writing four more novels :—

1880   *The Irrational Knot*   Published in serial form 1885-87.

1881   *Love Among the Artists*   ditto   1887-88.

1882   *Cashel Byron's Profession*   ditto   1885-86.

1883   *An Unsocial Socialist*   ditto   1884.
All five novels were rejected unanimously by the publishers of London and New York. Failure seemed complete and hopeless.

1884   He joined the Fabian Society 5th September and, with his new friend, Sidney Webb, made Socialism constitutional, practical and respectable as Fabianism. His first Fabian pamphlet appeared in the same year and is entitled *A Manifesto*.

1885   Started as a journalist on the reviewing staff (Books) of the *Pall Mall Gazette* at 2 guineas per column on May 16th (till 31.8.88). William Archer got him the job.
Made his first important public speech at the Industrial Remuneration Conference.
On 19th April his father died.

1886   William Archer again got him a job as Art Critic to *The World* (10.2.86—1.5.89).

1888   Began criticizing music for *The Star* under the pen name *Corno di Bassetto* (till 16.5.90).

1889   Edited *Fabian Essays* and contributed two of the essays.

1890   Left *The Star* and became Music Critic to *The World* (28.5.90—8.8.94). Five guineas a week.

1891	*Quintessence of Ibsenism* published.
1892	9th December, *Widowers' Houses*, his first play, performed in London by the Independent Theatre Society.
1893	*The Philanderer* and *Mrs. Warren's Profession* written, Shaw now deliberately adopting the profession of playwright.
1894	First performance of *Arms and the Man* in London and New York.
1895	Became Theatre Critic to *The Saturday Review* under the editorship of Frank Harris (5.1.95—21.5.98). Six guineas a week. Copyright performance of *Candida*.
1897	Became Vestryman in the Vestry of St. Pancras, London. *The Devil's Disciple*, a box office success with Richard Mansfield in New York, nets £2,000 for G.B.S. and makes it possible for him to marry. First performance of *Man of Destiny*.
1898	*Plays Pleasant* (*Arms and the Man*, *Candida*, *Man of Destiny*, *You Never Can Tell*) and *Unpleasant* (*Widowers' Houses*, *The Philanderer*, *Mrs. Warren's Profession*) published. On crutches following an injury and operation to his foot. On the 1st June at a London Registry Office married to Miss Charlotte Frances Payne-Townshend (Irish on her father's side, born 1857). Moved from 29 Fitzroy Square, his bachelor lodging for many years, to her flat in Adelphi Terrace (now demolished) and set up country quarters at Pitfold, Haslemere, changing later to Blen-cathra, Hindhead, then to Ruan Minor, Cornwall, again to Blackdown Cottage, near Haslemere, then to Pickards Cottage in Saint Katherines near Guildford in Surrey, from there to Maybury Knoll, Woking, then to the Old House above Welwyn in Hertfordshire, and finally in 1906 to the New Rectory in Ayot Saint Lawrence, which he bought and renamed Shaw's Corner. *The Perfect Wagnerite* written and published.
1899	Still on crutches but finished *Caesar and Cleopatra*. First performance of *You Never Can Tell*.
1900	First London performance of *Candida* and first production of *Captain Brassbound's Conversion* by the Stage Society.
1901	*Three Plays for Puritans* (*Devil's Disciple*, *Caesar and Cleopatra*, *Captain Brassbound's Conversion*) and *The Admirable Bashville* (dramatization of *Cashel Byron's Profession*) published.
1902	Wrote *Man and Superman* (published 1903).
1903	First full-dress performance of *The Admirable Bashville*.
1904	Defeated as Progressive Candidate for the South Saint Pancras seat on the London County Council. Wrote and published *The Commonsense of Municipal Trading* on his experiences as Vestryman and Borough Councillor until 1903, when he did not stand for re-election. The Vedrenne-Barker Season of (mainly) Shaw plays started at the Court Theatre, Sloane Square, London. *How He Lied To Her Husband* first performed in New York. *John Bull's Other Island* at the Court Theatre attracted a visit from King Edward VII and several Cabinet Ministers (1905), and established Shaw as a leading playwright in London as already in New York. *Candida* acted by Agnes Sorma established Shaw in the German Theatre.

1905	*The Philanderer* (first performance).
	First production of *Man and Superman*, minus the third act.
	Passion, Poison and Petrifaction produced in aid of the Actors' Orphanage (printed in *Translations and Tomfooleries*, 1926).
	Major Barbara at the Court Theatre (first performance).
1906	Gave sittings to Rodin for his bust. Moved to Ayot Saint Lawrence.
	First performance of *The Doctor's Dilemma* (published 1911) at the Court Theatre.
1907	*John Bull's Other Island*, *Major Barbara* and *How He Lied To Her Husband* published.
1908	*Getting Married* produced at the Haymarket Theatre, London.
	The Sanity of Art, contributed in 1895 to Benjamin Tucker's American journal *Liberty* in reply to Max Nordau's *Degeneration*, published as a book.
	Man and Superman produced in New York by Robert Loraine prodigiously lucrative for actor and author.
1909	*Press Cuttings* published and first performed at the Court Theatre.
	The Shewing Up Of Blanco Posnet first performed at the Abbey Theatre in Dublin (published 1911).
	Gave evidence before the Joint Select Committee on Dramatic Censorship.
1910	First performance of *Misalliance* (published 1914).
	First performance of *The Dark Lady of the Sonnets* (published 1914) in aid of the Shakespear Memorial Theatre.
1911	First performance of *Fanny's First Play* (published 1914).
1912	*Pygmalion* written. First produced in Vienna 1913, published 1916.
	First performance of *Overruled* (published 1916).
1913	February 19th, his Mother died.
	First performance of *Androcles and the Lion* (published 1916).
	First performance of *Great Catherine*.
1914	*The Music Cure* first performed (published 1926).
	Pygmalion a sensational success in London.
	November 14th, *Commonsense About the War* published.
1915	*Man and Superman* complete with *Don Juan in Hell*, performed for the first time.
1919	Published *Heartbreak House*, *Great Catherine* and *Playlets of the War* (*O'Flaherty, V.C.* ; *The Inca of Perusalem* ; *Augustus Does His Bit* ; *Annajanska, The Bolshevik Empress*).
1920	March 27th, his sister Lucy died.
	Back to Methuselah finished.
	Heartbreak House produced in America.
1921	First English performance of *Heartbreak House*.
	Back to Methuselah published.
1922	*Back to Methuselah* produced in America.

1923	*Jitta's Atonement*, an adaptation of a play by Siegfried Trebitsch, first performed in New York (published 1926).
	Wrote *St. Joan*.
1924	First English performance of *Back to Methuselah* in Birmingham.
	First performance of *St. Joan* in New York.
	First London production of *Back to Methuselah*.
	St. Joan first London production and publication.
	O'Flaherty, V.C., read by Shaw over the Wireless : his first broadcast.
1925	First public performance of *Mrs. Warren's Profession*, the Lord Chamberlain as Play Censor having vetoed previous attempts.
1926	*Passion, Poison and Petrifaction*, the first Shaw play broadcast in England as a play.
	July 26th, Seventieth birthday dinner at Hotel Metropole, Northumberland Avenue, London. Broadcast banned by Postmaster General.
	Received Nobel Prize for Literature for 1925.
1927	Left Adelphi Terrace for Whitehall Court, London, S.W.1.
	The Glimpse of Reality performed in London (published 1926).
1928	*The Intelligent Woman's Guide to Socialism and Capitalism* published.
	First London performance of *The Fascinating Foundling*, written in 1909. (Published 1926).
1929	Shaw Festival at Malvern, Worcestershire, opened with *The Apple Cart*. It had previously been performed in Warsaw.*
	The Apple Cart published.
1930	First volume of the Collected Edition of Shaw's works published (so far 33 volumes have appeared).
	Proposed the health of Albert Einstein at a banquet in Einstein's honour held at Savoy Hotel, London, on October 28th.
1931	Visit to Russia with Lord and Lady Astor and Lord Lothian. Received by Stalin. Celebrated his 75th birthday in Moscow.
	The Ellen Terry-Shaw correspondence (1892-1922) published.
	December 29th, G.B.S. and Mrs. Shaw sailed for Cape Town.
1932	*Too True to be Good* first performed in Boston, Mass.; first performance in England at Malvern.
	December 16th, Mr. and Mrs. Shaw went on tour around the world on The Empress of Britain. He lectured in New York under the auspices of the American Academy of Political Science.
	The Adventures of the Black Girl in Her Search for God published.
1933	First performance of *On the Rocks* in London. (Published 1934).
1934	*Village Wooing* first performed (published 1934).
	Too True to be Good published.
	First production of *The Six of Calais* (published 1936).
	Visit to New Zealand of Mr. and Mrs. Shaw.

* The reason that several first performances did not take place in England was that continental theatre managers complained that the hostile English criticisms reported by the news agencies damaged them and that they must have the first bite. Shaw complied.

1935	20th June, became Freeman of City of London (as member of the City Company of Stationers and Newspaper Makers). G.B.S. and Mrs. Shaw left for a tour around South Africa. Malvern Festival opened with English Première of *The Simpleton of the Unexpected Isles* (published 1936). The first production was by the Theatre Guild in New York.
1936	*The Millionairess* published. It was first performed on the Continent. First English production by The Forsyth Players in Bexhill. Sailed with his wife on board S.S. *Arandora Star* (Pacific Cruise). 3rd July registered as Citizen of the Irish Free State but retained his British Nationality.
1937	*Cymbeline Refinished* (a new last Act for Shakespeare's play) written for Stratford Festival but performed only in London.
1938	Ill with anaemia. *Cymbeline Refinished* published. World Première of *Geneva* at Malvern. *Pygmalion* filmed by Gabriel Pascal.
1939	*In Good King Charles' Golden Days* produced at Malvern, and published with Topolski drawings. *Geneva* published with Topolski drawings.
1940	*Major Barbara* filmed by Pascal.
1941	On his 85th birthday *The Shaw Society* founded in London.
1943	12th September, Mrs. Shaw died. Finished *Everybody's Political What's What*? (published 1944).
1944	*Shaw's Corner* given to the National Trust. Clara and Harry Higgs (housekeeper and gardener) retired; and Mrs. Alice Laden became " manager of my last home."
1945	*Caesar and Cleopatra* filmed by Pascal. Shaw's Irish property municipalized by special Act of Parliament of Eire.
1946	90th birthday: Special performance of *Don Juan in Hell* at the Arts Theatre, London. Shaw Exhibition at the National Book League. Received Honorary Freedom of Dublin. First Honorary Freeman of the Metropolitan Borough of St. Pancras. *Back to Methuselah* published with new Postscript as No. 500 in the *World's Classics* series by the Oxford University Press.
1947	*Geneva* published with a new Act. Statue of St. Joan erected in the grounds of *Shaw's Corner*. Finished new play, " a Comedy of No Manners." Plaque unveiled on December 6th at Torca Cottage, Dalkey, his boyhood summer home.
1948	At work on a collection of autobiographical sketches.

F. E. LOEWENSTEIN.

Bernard Shaw's Ancestors and Relations

Robert Shaw (great-great-grand-father) of Sandpits, Co. Kilkenny, who married Mary Markham.

Mary Markham, sister of the Archbishop of York and great-great-grandmother of G.B.S.

Frances Shaw (grandmother).

Bernard Shaw (grandfather).
Solicitor, of Dublin.

Mr. and Mrs. George Carr Shaw
(Father and Mother).

Mrs. Shaw (Mother) in 1897.

A much later photograph taken by
G.B.S. of his Mother.

An early photo of his Mother (left)
and his Father (right) with George
John Vandaleur Lee, "conductor of
genius" in the middle. Photographed
by Richard Pigott, forger of the so-
called Parnell letters. The figure in
the sombrero is Charles Cummins, a
noted amateur tenor and musical
colleague of Mrs. Shaw.

Sir Robert Shaw, the second Baronet.
(*Painting by Henry Pickersgill*).

R. F. Shaw (Uncle Frederick) 1863.

Sir Frederick Shaw, Bart., Recorder
of Dublin.

Sir Eyre Massey Shaw, a distantly
related " Cork Shaw," Captain of
the London Fire Brigade, celebrated
in a Gilbert & Sullivan opera.

19

Charlotte Johnston (Aunt Chah)
paternal aunt.

Shaw's uncle Edward whom he
never saw. He emigrated, and
founded the Australian Shaws, now
a numerous clan.

Walter Bagenal Gurly, his maternal
Grandfather.

J. H. Whitcroft, 1862, "Uncle
John," brother of G.B.S.'s maternal
grandmother.

Walter John Gurly (maternal uncle) 1874.

The Rev. William George Carroll (paternal uncle), Rector of St. Bride's, Dublin, taught him his Latin Grammar.

Matthew Edward McNulty and G.B.S. (1874) (the earliest photograph of Shaw).

Elinor Agnes Shaw (Sister Yuppy) 1874 (died 1876).

G.B.S., aged 20, April, 1876, at Ventnor.

G.B.S. and John Thomas Gibbings, 1876.

Robert Moore Fishbourne and G.B.S., 1876.

Lucy (sister) and G.B.S., Ventnor, 1876.

His sister Lucy, first-born of the family " whom everybody loved and who loved nobody."

G.B.S., 1879.

Horace Payne-Townshend (father-in-law).

Lottie Payne-Townshend (later, Mrs. G.B.S.)

No. 1, Hatch Street, Dublin, residence of the Lee-Shaw joint household.

The birthplace of G.B.S. on the 26th July 1856, at 33 Synge Street, Dublin, then 3 Upper Synge Street.

Plaque unveiled December 6th, 1947.

Torca Cottage, Dalkey, where G.B.S. spent his boyhood.

Rutland Avenue, Dolphin's Barn, Dublin, with the shop attached to the mill held by Clibborn and Shaw.

Bushy Park, Rathfarnham, family seat of the Dublin Shaws.

St. Pancras Town Council in session, 1900, with G.B.S. at this end of the table on the right.

May Morris, Halliday Sparling, (Sir) Emery Walker and G.B.S.

Keir Hardie Mrs. Shaw   G.B.S.

G.B.S.'s first flight at Hendon, in the early days of air travel.

Shaw the Orator, by
Bertha Newcombe.

(*right*)

Mr. Shaw's friend, Alvin
Langdon Coburn, a famous
photographer, photographed
by G.B.S.

(*above*)

1898. At Blen-Cathra on Hind-head, part of St. Edmund's College.

(*below*)

Three snaps in 1898, the year he married, the first as a beggar whilst still on crutches.

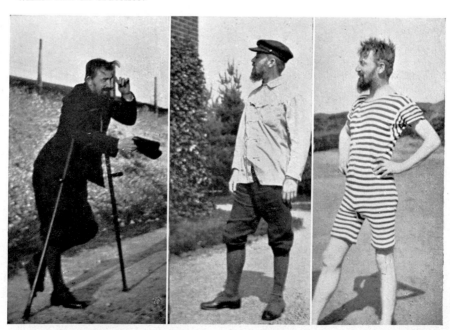

(*left*)

1888. At ease in summer in Battersea Park.

(*below*)

1898. At work in winter on Hindhead.

Mrs. Shaw smiling, a rare picture, as she hated being photographed.

Dining on vegetables in great splendour of silver plate in Derry, County Cork, his wife's birthplace.

(left)

Mrs. Bernard Shaw in the first year of her marriage.　Photo by G.B.S.

G.B.S. newly married and lame, in his invalid chair at Pitfold, the home of Lord Beveridge.

(*left*)

A fine portrait by Alvin Langdon Coburn.

(*below*)

A picture taken at a Fabian Summer School.

On January 7th, 1914, John Jasper was tried by the Dickens Fellowship for the murder of Edwin Drood at the King's Hall, Covent Garden. In this picture of the jury the figures are, from left to right (front row), Sir Edward Russell, W. W. Jacobs, Pett Ridge, Arthur Morrison, Francesco Berger, Tom Gallon and Bernard Shaw (foreman) ; (back row), Coulson Kernahan, Ridgwell Cullum, William de Morgan, Justin Huntly McCarthy, William Archer and Thomas Seccombe.

G.B.S. writing *Cæsar and Cleopatra*.

AYOT ST LAWRENCE . WELWYN . HERTS

STATION: WHEATHAMPSTEAD. L. & N. E. R. 2¼ MILES

TELEGRAMS: BERNARD SHAW . CODICOTE.

4 . WHITEHALL COURT . LONDON . S . W . I .

IN LOVING REMEMBRANCE
OF MARY ANN SOUTH,
WHO DIED IN LONDON
AND WAS BROUGHT HERE TO REST
BY HER CHILDREN
BORN MARCH 5 1825
DIED FEBRUARY 13 1895
IN THE MIDST OF LIFE WE ARE IN
DEATH

HER TIME WAS SHORT

Inscription in the churchyard
at Ayot St Laurence — the
classical church.

This inscription, copied by G.B.S., made him decide to
live at Ayot Saint Lawrence, where 70 years is considered
a short life.

(*left*)

The hatstand just inside the door at Ayot Saint Lawrence.

With Gabriel Pascal in the garden at Ayot Saint Lawrence.

A view of the garden.

The view from the window of Shaw's bedroom at Ayot Saint Lawrence.

Mrs. Higgs, for many years housekeeper at Ayot.

Mr. Higgs, the gardener.

Shaw sits by Prince Paul Troubetzkoy's sculpture of a lamb.

(*left*)

Reporters and cameramen wishing to see G.B.S. apply to his housekeeper, Mrs. Alice Laden.

(*below*)

G.B.S., a keen motorist for 30 years, drove his own Rolls Royce.

Alfred Drury, assistant gardener at Shaw's Corner, welcomed back there after his military service in 1939-45.

Francis William Day, veteran of the 1914-18 war, since then G.B.S's head gardener and chauffeur, described by him as A Treasure.

(left)

Shaw is an ardent photographer and is often to be seen in the garden taking pictures.

(below)

A group outside the village Church after a musical hour. Miss Beryl Ireland, G.B.S., the Rector (The Rev. A. C. V. de Candole), Mr. John Hunt and his mother.

(left)
Complete with a miner's helmet he saws logs.

(below)
Mr. Shaw takes a walk with his bibliographer and remembrancer, Dr. F. E. Loewenstein.

(left)

After a fall in London in 1946, G.B.S. is soon walking in his garden again.

(below)

At work in the garden shelter where much of his work has been written.

(left)

Mr. Shaw at the village post office with Mrs. Jisbella Lyth, the postmistress.

(below)

On the mantelpiece in Shaw's drawing room stands a crockery image of Shakespear. Above hangs an early portrait of Mrs. Shaw by Sartorio.

(*left*)

G.B.S. at his London flat.

(*bottom left*)

The air raid warden at White-hall Court presents Mr. Shaw with his plastic helmet.

(*bottom right*)

Admiring the blue delphin-iums on his 90th birthday

(left)

In bakelite helmet and cape, Mr. Shaw is well prepared in 1940.

(below)

Miss Margaret Cashin, the Irish housemaid, receives the Shavian post through the kitchen window.

(left)

Another photo of his revolving summer house, where on the steps he sometimes reads a book.

(below)

The village girls wait to greet Mr. Shaw on his 90th birthday.

(*left*)

G.B.S. looks at London from the balcony of his flat in Whitehall Court.

(*below*)

Shaw is vitally interested in Russia and is seen here reading " U.S.S.R. in Construction."

(*left*)

G.B.S. in an enquiring mood.

(*below*)

Playing his clavicord.

(left)

With Miss Blanche Patch, private secretary since 1920.

(below)

At Malvern, Ellen Pollock's son is interested in Shaw's camera (1934).

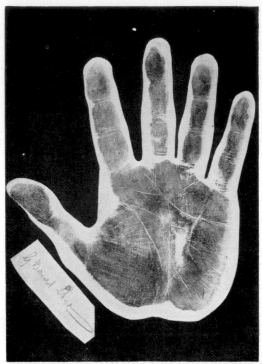

(left)

This picture shows Mr. Shaw's palm, suitably inked to strengthen the lines.

(below)

A picture taken as G.B.S. corrects a page of MS.

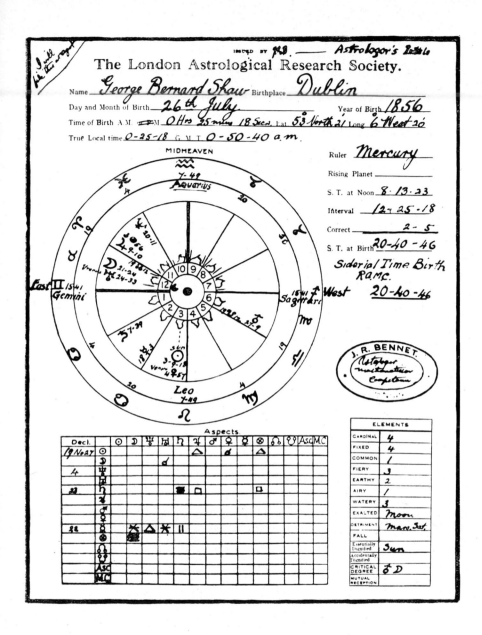

Shaw's Horoscope, worked out by a Cape Town Astrologer.

53

(left)

Mr. Shaw at Dubrovnik (Ragusa) in 1929.

(below)

Sunbathing at Cap d' Antibes.

(*left*)

In Manila, Bernard Shaw was entertained by Governor Theodore Roosevelt in 1933.

(*right*)

The face behind the mask is that of G.B.S. This photograph was taken in Tokyo in 1933.

(left)

Bernard Shaw learning the tango in Madeira.

(below)

The world famous playright is welcomed to the Country of the Rising Sun by Isho Abe.

(left)

G.B.S. on holiday in unusual attire.

(below)

Shaw's reception at Moscow.

(*left*)

Mr. and Mrs. Bernard Shaw leaving Whitehall Court for New Zealand, in 1934.

(*below*)

G.B.S. in the Parthenon with a group of Greek pressmen who came to interview him.

(left)

A spritely walk shaded from the sun.

(below)

At the hot springs in Rotorua, New Zealand, 1934, with his guide.

MAN
AND
SUPER
-MAN·
=

ALL the WORLD's A STAGE·SOCIETY·

DESIGN FOR A STATUE OF "JOHN BULL'S OTHER PLAYWRIGHT."
After certain hints by "G.B.S."

(*left*)

A clever caricature by E. T. Reed, which appeared in *Punch*.

(*right*)

One of Max Beerbohm's early caricatures of " G. B. Shaw in his element."

(left)

A delightful caricature by Low.

(right)

From an envelope which arrived safely at Shaw's flat in London.

TO →

LONDON

OR - WHERE - EVER - HE - HAPPENS - TO · BE · AT · THE · MOMENT!

(*left*)

Sigmund Strobl's bust of Shaw.

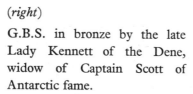

(*right*)

G.B.S. in bronze by the late Lady Kennett of the Dene, widow of Captain Scott of Antarctic fame.

A well-known portrait.

Mr. Shaw at the gate of Shaw's Corner.

Portrait of G.B.S. by Augustus John with the aged original

(*left*)

Bernard Shaw by Prince Paul Troubetzkoy (1926).

(*right*)

Troubetzkoy's life-size statue of Shaw, in the National Gallery of Ireland.

(*left*)

The Hon. John Collier with his portrait of Shaw, rejected by the Royal Academy in 1927, now in the National Gallery of Ireland.

(*right*)

G.B.S. associated with Anatole France, in a stained glass window portraying Joan of Arc in the Ethical Church, Bayswater.

(*left*)

A portrait taken in 1919.

(*below*)

Mr. Shaw, the bust and the Sculptor—Jo Davidson.

(*left*)

G.B.S. at the Fitzwilliam Museum in 1935.

(*below*)

An amusing drawing of G.B.S. and G.K.C. (Gilbert Keith Chesterton) as Don Quixote and Sancho Panza.

DON QUIXOTE, SANCHO PANZA, AND THE SHEEP

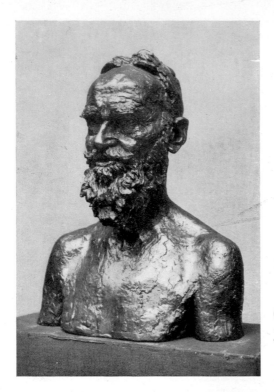

(left)

Jacob Epstein's bust of Shaw.

(right)

A fine portrait by Karsh of Ottawa.

(*left*)

Rodin at work on his bust of Shaw.

(*below*)

Sava arranging his bust of Shaw at The Leicester Galleries in 1938.

(*left*)

Portrait, 1937.

(*right*)

An earlier portrait by Lena Connell.

(*left*)

Miss Lilian Browne with the Augustus John portrait of G.B.S., "The Sleeping Philosopher," which is owned by H.M. The Queen.

(*below*)

"I dreamt St. Peter sat for his portrait," by Fred. Elwell, R.A., caused much controversy in 1947, because of the likeness of St. Peter to Bernard Shaw.

(*left*)
Another Alvin Langdon Coburn portrait of G.B.S.

Howard Coster's composite picture of great men of our time

The real G.B.S. assisting Edgar
Norfolk with make-up at the
rehearsal of " Spacetime Inn."

Queen Victoria and G.B.S.
impersonated in " Spacetime
Inn," by Lionel Britton.

A photograph of one of Feliks Topolski's oil paintings of Shaw.

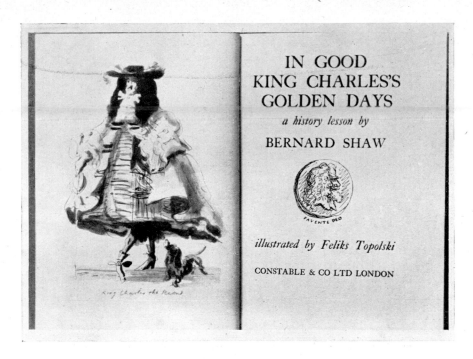

Frontispiece and Title Page.

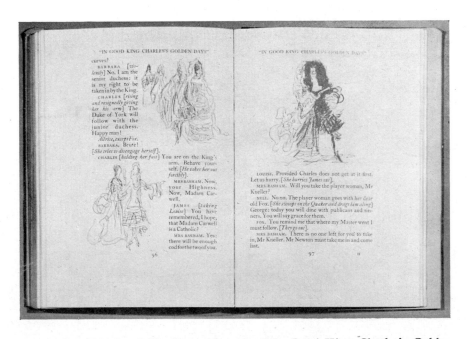

Some of Feliks Topolski's illustrations for " In Good King Charles's Golden Days," with two pages of text.

The frontispiece and title page of Feliks Topolski's Shaw book.

Shaw's own suggestion to John Farleigh for an illustration in *The Black Girl*. The flying Irishman is Mr. Shaw himself. See next page.

John Farleigh's masterly version of Shaw's suggestion on the preceding
page.

(*left*)

An unusual picture of G.B.S. playing tennis with Albert Coates, the well-known conductor, on the shore of Lago Maggiore.

(*below*)

G.B.S. at Malvern Festival with (L. to R.) Scott Sunderland, Margaret Chatwin, Gwen ffrangçon Davies, Phyllis Neilson Terry and Aubrey Mallalieu.

The famous American blind deaf mute, Hellen Keller, G.B.S. and Lady Astor.

A broadcast interview with Mr. Maurice Webb at Durban, 1935.

(*left*)

G.B.S. at rehearsals of Rutland Boughton's Opera *The Lily Maid* at Glastonbury in 1937, with Miss Sybil Evers and Mr. Arthur Fear.

A unique trio commemorating the Shaw-Chesterton debate with Hilaire Belloc in the chair.

(left)

Albert Coates and Shaw after a recording at The Gramophone Co's works at Hayes.

(below)

G.B.S. visits Margaret Mac-Millan's Nursery at Deptford in the East End of London.

(*left*)

Shaw at the opening of the Village Hall, Kelmscott, Lechlade, Gloucestershire, in memory of William Morris (1934).

Sir Whitworth Wallis and Sir Robert Vansittart, with G.B.S., who was given the title deeds of the projected site of The National Theatre at South Kensington, London.

Gene Tunney, former American Heavyweight Title-holder on holiday with G.B.S. at Brioni, island in the Adriatic.

G.B.S. with Gene Tunney, Mrs. Tunney and the great German surgeon who arrived miraculously in Brione just in time to save her life when Gene prayed for divine aid.

Lawrence Tompkins, American sculptor who arrived in England with a design for a giant monument to G.B.S., and his wife Molly Tompkins at a Summer School.

G.B.S. and Sean O'Casey.

Barrie, Galsworthy, Shaw and Granville-Barker.

G.B.S. and H. G. Wells.

(*left*)

Shaw in Malvern as patron saint of the Festival looks the part.

Cliveden, country seat of the Astors, where G.B.S. met many distinguished guests during his visits before the death of Mrs. Shaw in 1943.

(*left*)

Shaw explains a new camera to Miss Ellen Pollock and Mr. Ernest Thesiger at Malvern.

(*below*)

At the 1932 Malvern Festival.
Top row: (left to right) Tony Marshall, Gudrun Mayer, Harold Knight, Scott Sunderland, Mrs. J. T. Grein.
Second row: George Bishop, Tanya Moiseiwitsch, Daisy Kennedy Drinkwater, Bibby Byrne, Dame Laura Knight.
Bottom row: J. T. Grein, Robert de Smet, G. B. Shaw, John Drinkwater, Earl of Sandwich, Sir Barry Jackson.

(*left*)

Shaw with Feliks Topolski at an exhibition of the artist's works.

(*below*)

Lunacharsky, Stanislavski and G.B.S. at a Literary and Scientific Club in a hunting lodge near Moscow.

(*left*)

Lady Gregory with her grandson, photographed at Coole by G.B.S. They were close friends. He called her the Irish Molière.

John Pentland Mahaffy, famous Provost of Trinity College, Dublin, historian and friend of kings and celebrities, photographed by G.B.S., in Sir Horace Plunkett's garden in Foxrock.

Lady Scott, born Kathleen Bruce, widow of the Antarctic explorer, later Lady Kennet of The Dene, eminent sculptress, at Ayot Saint Lawrence.

(left)

Lady Astor with G.B.S. on his 73rd birthday.

(below)

Charles Chaplin, Shaw and Lord and Lady Astor at the first night of " City Lights" in London.

(*left*)

Dame Clara Butt entertains the author at Monte Carlo.

(*below*)

Amy Johnson, Charles Chaplin, Lady Astor and G.B.S. at St. James's Square, in 1931.

Claire Sheridan and her daughter with G.B.S., Mrs. Clifford Sharpe (Rosamund Bland) and Clifford Sharpe at the Russian Embassy.

Gabriel Pascal, Bernard Shaw, Leslie Howard and Lady Oxford at Pinewood studios.

A curious picture. Lord Howard de Walden, William Archer, Sir James Barrie, G.K. Chesterton and G.B.S., cowboys in a discarded film by Barrie.

Mr. and Mrs. Pember Reeves with Mrs. Shaw at Pickards Cottage, Saint Katherines, near Guildford, in 1901. Photo by G.B.S. Pember Reeves, later Principal of the London School of Economics, was then High Commissioner for New Zealand.

T. E. Lawrence (Lawrence of Arabia), friend of the Shaws. His Memorial at
St. Martin's, Wareham, Dorset.

Miss Harriet Cohen, pianist and friend.

May Morris, "The Mystical Betrothed."

Mrs. Patrick Campbell, the great actress in her bed at 13 Kensington Square, in London.   Photo by G.B.S.

The late Henry S. Salt, Shelleyan Humanitarian and author of an autobiography entitled *Seventy Years Among Savages* Shaw's host for many summers.

Rainer Maria Rilke, Austrian Poet and Rodin's Secretary in 1906 when G.B.S. sat for his bust daily for a month in the Château des Brilliants at Meudon.

At Cliveden in 1928 with Lord Astor.

Graham Wallas, one of the witnesses at Shaw's wedding, eminent University Extension lecturer and Fabian Essayist.

H. G. Wells.

Hubert Bland, Fabian.

Henry Halliday Sparling, May
Morris's husband, son-in-law of
William Morris.

Ernest Belfort Bax, philosopher
and one of the founders of Marxist
Socialism in England.   Arnold
Bax's uncle.

Harley Granville-Barker, Playwright, Actor, Producer of Shakespeare unabridged, and author of treaties on Shakespearean production.

Henry Hyde Champion, Editor of *Today* in which some of Shaw's early novels were first printed. Began as youngest adjutant in the British Army in Afghanistan.

John Burns, the Man with the Red Flag, afterwards the first artisan to become a Cabinet Minister.

Henry Mayers Hyndman, Marxist founder of the Social-Democratic Federation. Said by Shaw to have " a striking resemblance to God."

Frank Harris, Shaw's chosen editor in 1895, and author of a Shaw biography.

William Morris, Craftsman, Poet, Socialist.

Siegfried Trebitsch, Shaw's devoted Austrian translator.

Edith Craig, Ellen Terry's daughter.

William Archer, Scot, critic, and translator of Ibsen, who launched Shaw on his journalistic career.

Sir Barry Jackson with Shaw at Bath.

Miss Ellen Terry in 1883.

Edward R. Pease, Father of the
Fabian Society.

Elgar rehearsing his Nursery Suite in 1931. G.B.S. on his left. The Duke
and Duchess of York, now King and Queen of the British Commonwealth, on
his right. The Suite is dedicated to the two royal children. Elgar and Shaw
became intimate friends. Elgar's Severn Suite is dedicated to Shaw.

Sir Edward Elgar and Shaw at Malvern.

Mrs. Shaw and Roy Limbert, manager
of the Malvern Festival Theatre.

Professor Albert Einstein, Lord Rothschild and Shaw at the dinner organised
by the Ort-Oze Committee at the Savoy Hotel, London, in 1930.

(*left*)

Sidney Webb in 1932 at Ayot Saint Lawrence. Photo by G.B.S.

Beatrice Webb, photographed by G.B.S. She and her husband, his Fabian colleagues, were also his dearest friends. He claimed their interment in Westminster Abbey.

Mrs. Shaw's sister, Mrs. Mary Cholmondeley (Sissy) for whom G.B.S. wrote *The Intelligent Woman's Guide to Socialism and Capitalism*.

Edstaston's ancient church, in Shropshire, containing a window dedicated to The Intelligent Woman by her widower. Both are buried there.

(*above*)   Miss Mary Farmer, the original of Louisa
Straker in *Man and Superman*, photographed
at Pickards Cottage by G.B.S. She was
cook and housekeeper for years in the Shaw
household.   Though attractive enough to
justify the infatuation of Mendoza in the
play she died unmarried.

Miss Blanche Patch, Secretary to
G.B.S. since 1920.

Prof. Archibald Henderson, Shaw's
American biographer, a noted mathe-
matician.

G.B.S. with his biographer Hesketh Pearson in 1945.

Friend Ivo Currall has a rest with Bernard Shaw who has been sawing wood.

Dr. William Maxwell conducts G.B.S. around the 90th Birthday Exhibition at the National Book League, London.

Dean Inge and Mr. Shaw on their Hellenic Cruise. Shaw calls this picture The Temptation.

Bernard Shaw receives the freedom of the City of Dublin at Ayot in 1946.
(L. to R.) F. E. Loewenstein, The City Manager of Dublin, The Irish High
Commissioner in London, The City Manager's Clerk.

Mr. High Commissioner Dulanty receives the MSS of Shaw's novels for the
National Library of Ireland.

(left)

Bernard Shaw at the Regent's Park Open-Air Theatre, 1934.

At a rehearsal in Regent's Park of " The Six of Calais." Phyllis Neilson Terry and Charles Carson talking to G.B.S.

Charles McEvoy. Playwright who died young, brother of the painter, Ambrose McEvoy, and son of Captain McEvoy, whose profession of inventing war weapons suggested that of Captain Shotover in *Heartbreak House*. Photographed by G.B.S.

Sir Sydney Carlyle Cockerell, intimate friend of Ruskin, William Morris, Wilfred Blunt and Shaw. Curator and developer of the Fitzwilliam Museum in Cambridge.
Photo by G.B.S.

Sir John Squire at Barrow House on Derwentwater with G.B.S. in 1915 at a Fabian Conference there.

BARRY SULLIVAN
1821—1891

Successor to Macready, and
last of the line of mighty Shakespearean actors that began with
Burbage. A stage Superman,
the idol of G.B.S's boyhood.
Born in Birmingham.   Irish
parentage.   Father a Waterloo
veteran.   Began in Cork.

SIR HENRY IRVING
John Henry Brodribb
1838—1905

30 years leading London
actor-manager. G.B.S's great
disappointment.   He says
Irving missed his two golden
chances : Ibsen and Shaw, and
mutilated Shakespear.   A
Somerset man : first English
actor to be knighted.   Buried
in Westminster Abbey.

Charles Charrington, the original Mr. Bohun, Q.C., in *You Never Can Tell.*

Sir Johnston Forbes-Robertson in The Devil's Disciple, 1900

G.B.S. as the Beadle during a rehearsal of *Getting Married*.

Shaw rehearsing a scene from *Androcles and the Lion* with Lillah McCarthy and Harley Granville-Barker.

SAINT JOAN

Sybil Thorndike for whom the part of Saint Joan was written.

The Statue of Jehanne by Clare Winsten which stands in Shaw's garden at Ayot Saint Lawrence.

Lillah McCarthy (Lady Keeble). Creator of many of Shaw's dramatic characters, notably Ann Whitefield in *Man and Superman*.

G.B.S. at Newcastle to see an amateurs' performance of his play *Candida*. He is shown talking to Miss Edith Bulmer and Sir Charles Trevelyan.

The neon lights on Broadway, New York.

Rex Harrison, Robert Morley, G.B.S. and Pascal at the Albert Hall.

G.B.S. and Wendy Hiller during a luncheon to inaugurate the filming of
" Pygmalion."

Robert Morley, Wendy Hiller, G.B.S., Miss Patch and Gabriel Pascal.

G.B.S., Claude Rains (Cæsar) and Gabriel Pascal before the filming of *Cæsar and Cleopatra.*

G.B.S. tries a roman helmet for the benefit of Pascal.

Gabriel Pascal studies a model
of Cleopatra . . . .

and discusses the film with Vivien Leigh and G.B.S.

G.B.S. invites Gabriel Pascal into his summer house to discuss the filming of *Cæsar and Cleopatra*.

He listens to Georges Auric playing some of the music specially written for the film.

A joke with Apollodorus (Stewart Granger) and Rufio (Basil Sydney).

G.B.S. has a walk in the garden at Ayot St. Lawrence with Vivien Leigh and Gabriel Pascal.

List of Pictures and Credits

The photograph on the book jacket is by Karsh of Ottawa.